IMAGES
of America

WASHINGTON COUNTY
MISSISSIPPI

Riverdale Plantation was built about 1850 by Dr. Robert J. Turnbull. This well-known plantation covered more than 1,500 acres of prime cotton land and was bought from Dr. Turnbull by the W.H. Brown family in 1900. Because of new levee construction to the east of the house, Riverdale has been moved several times. The house was rolled on logs to its present location by one harnessed mule with a hemp rope. Later, Ed and Cornelia Brown Touchberry and their family owned this beautiful old plantation.

IMAGES
of America

WASHINGTON COUNTY
MISSISSIPPI

Russell S. Hall, Princella W. Nowell, and Stacy Childress

ARCADIA
PUBLISHING

Published by Arcadia Publishing
Charleston, South Carolina

Library of Congress Catalog Card Number: 00-108020

For all general information contact Arcadia Publishing at:
Telephone 843-853-2070
Fax 843-853-0044
E-mail sales@arcadiapublishing.com
For customer service and orders:
Toll-Free 1-888-313-2665

Visit us on the Internet at www.arcadiapublishing.com

ACKNOWLEDGMENTS

The authors—Russell S. Hall of Germantown, TN; Princella W. Nowell of Greenville, MS; and Stacy Childress of Madison, MS—wish to thank the following for their assistance in the creation of this book:
Katie Sims—Glen Allan, MS; Frank Youngblood—Jackson, MS; Peggy A. Hall—Memphis, TN; Winnie Darnell—Glen Allan, MS; Rob Roy Fisher—Greenville, MS; Paul Love—Glen Allan, MS; South Carolina Department of Archives and History—Charleston, SC; Elizabeth Wesson—Glen Allan, MS; T.C. Woods—Jackson, MS; Mr. and Mrs. Buddy McKamy—Chatham, MS; John Allen Darnell—Glen Allan, MS; M.R. Williams II—Greenville, MS; Mrs. Henry C. Tucker—Greenville, MS; Emogene McIntyer—Doddsville, MS; Robert Phillips—Dallas, TX; Katherine Myers Pearson—Rosedale, MS; Memphis Public Library—Memphis, TN; Mr. and Mrs. John Bridges—Glen Allan, MS; Jenny and Anne Bratton—Hollandale, MS; Elizabeth R. Mann—Oxford, MS; Nell Porter Hencey—Jackson, AL; Lynda Speaks—Madison, MS; Nell Finley—Lafayette, IN; Mrs. William J. Shutt—Hollandale, MS; Mississippi Archives and History—Jackson, MS; Thomas Worthington—Beach Grove, TN; Mrs. Sidney Law—Glen Allan, MS; and E.V. Richardson—Madison, MS.

The following individuals and organizations have provided photographs for this publication. Throughout the text, they will be identified by initials that appear in parentheses.

Princella Wilkerson Nowell (PWN); Kristen Nowell (KN); Gordon Cotton (OCM); Kay Clanton, director of the William A. Percy Library (WAP); William Payne (WP); Kathy Eubank (KE); Marlowe Park Jr. (MP); Mary Lynn Powers (MLP); Gloria Campbell (GTC); Ralph Owen (RO); Bill Weilenman (BW); Delta Branch Experiment Station (DBES); Don O. Baker (DOB); Karen Swain (KS); Davis Nunnery (DN); Bern Keating (BK); Frank England (FE); Anne Rayner (AR); Kenneth Haxton (KH); John Keen (JK); Butch Ruth (BR); Leland Historic Foundation (LHF); Greenville Compress (GC); Paul Artman Jr.(PA); and Broughton Henderson (BH); Sharon Neff (SN); Jessica Brent (JB); Eden Brent (EB); Arthur Novell (AN); William Saratt (WS); Warren Dawson (WD); and R.D.L. (RDL).

CONTENTS

INTRODUCTION

Cane breaks, floods, and bears! Oh my!

Mississippi had already joined the Union when the Choctaw chiefs signed the Treaty of Doak's Stand with the United States in 1820. During the course of the years that followed the signing, the Choctaw people would be removed from their land to Indian Territory west of the Mississippi River, the New Purchase would be surveyed for sale, and, finally, in 1827 the boundaries for Washington County, Mississippi would be drawn. The original size of the county equaled the state of Delaware, and its boundaries included parts of modern-day Bolivar, Sunflower, Humphreys, Sharkey, and Issaquena Counties.

Prior to the Choctaws, a pre-contact tribe of Native Americans roamed "the Swamp." Referred to as the "Mississippians" for their cultural similarities to other groups found on sites along the Mississippi River, these people built earthen mounds for ceremonial and burial purposes. In northwest Washington County the Mississippians left a site that today still contains fifteen mounds; the largest of which is 55 feet, or five and a half stories high. The mounds on this site are a bizarre contrast to the low, flat land that surrounds them.

The Mississippi River, a "super" highway both in the past and in the present, borders Washington County on the west. Settlers and speculators knew that the highest ground (140 feet) was along the natural levee near the river; the land east of the natural levee was lower (130 feet). This land consisted of undrained swamps, cane breaks, and sloughs interrupted only by the high banks of Deer Creek. Before the good drainage practices of the 20th century, this low land was subject to flooding. Still further east the land falls away again to the Bogue Swamp (125 feet).

Pioneers and speculators came to Washington County seeking its rich soil, and the first plantations were situated either on the Mississippi River or had stream access to it. Landings were named for plantation owners or had some association to the state from which the landowners originated. On the north, at the Bolivar County line, is Offutt Landing. As one continues downstream, there are Woodstock, belonging to the Carter family of Virginia, and Argyle Landing, owned by the W.R. Campbell family. Island 83 in front of Greenville was also named Sutton's Island. Below Greenville are Warfield Point, Kentucky Bend in the Mississippi River, Worthington Point, and Princeton Landing. Carolina Landing and Valewood straddle the modern county line between Issaquena and Washington Counties.

Among the names of the better-known early settlers on Lake Washington are Wade Hampton and Robert Turnbull, both of South Carolina, and the Johnsons, Wards, Erwins, and Clarks, all of Kentucky. On Deer Creek were the Percy, Lee, Paxton, Dixon, Rucks, Fall, and Yerger families. Williams Bayou families included the Perkins, Mosby, and Ireys families.

The original inhabitants of Washington County built mounds a mile south of Winterville more than 1,000 years ago and used them as ceremonial centers. Unfortunately, modern citizens have plowed many of them down, although now their educational and recreational values are becoming more realized. (WAP.)

Most of the early homes in the region were log cabins. Just preceding the War between the States, an era of large home building took place. Two homes that survived the war, time, and fires are the Greek-revival-style Belmont and the Italianate Mount Holly. Junius Ward's log cabin on Lake Washington is the oldest house in the county. Wildwood Plantation on the southern limit of present-day Greenville is the second-oldest home and is the most typical of the county's early architecture. A scattering of lesser-known early homes can be found throughout the county.

Absentee landholders Stephen Duncan and Henry Vick had homes in Natchez and in Vicksburg, respectively. These proprietors hired overseers to work the land and spent only the fall and winter months on their plantations in the Swamp. Mosquitoes, along with the humidity, made the summer months almost unbearable.

Any small plantation consisted of at least 1,000 acres of which one half or less was cultivated. The rest of the land was covered with timber, and each year a few more acres were cleared. Floodwaters covered the Swamp during April and May. There was no man-made barrier to hold back the annual floods of the alluvial plain, so the planting of cotton and corn with mule and oxen began as soon as the threat of overflow had passed. Work continued throughout the summer to the fall harvest and ginning time. Steamboats carried the bales of cotton downriver to New Orleans and passengers north to Memphis.

In the Swamp, the only towns, which were little more than landings and shipping ports for crops, were county seats. Washington County's first county seat, New Mexico, caved into the river, and in 1830, Princeton became the new seat of government. At an early date, a railroad was planned to originate from Princeton and return with crops from the Deer Creek area, but the failure of the Mississippi Banks resulted in this rail line never being built. Caving also caused Princeton's removal as the county seat. In 1847, Greenville, named for a friend of George Washington, was established. Its growth and success relied upon its being a port for settlers on upper Deer Creek. If strong levees could be built to protect the crops around Greenville, there would be no richer place to live than Washington County.

In 1858, a great levee-building scheme was created. The plan was to build a continuous, 200-mile "wall" along the Mississippi River from the Chickasaw Bluffs in Memphis to Walnut Hills in Vicksburg. Several levees were constructed, but with the outbreak of war, the work was abandoned and many levees were destroyed or fell into disrepair. By the end of the Mexican

War, the population of the Swamp had increased, but after the War between the States, many left never to return to the land that was so susceptible to flooding. Because there was no wealth in the country, it took almost ten years to bring the levees to a semi-stable condition. Once again, people felt safe enough to live in Washington County. For practical reasons the decision was made to stop calling the area the Swamp and rename it "the Delta," the shortened name for the Yazoo-Mississippi Delta.

Federal troops destroyed "Old" Greenville, and "new" Greenville was established just 1 mile to the north of the original town in 1865. Five years later, when Mississippi rejoined the Union, Greenville was incorporated. A fire in September 1874 destroyed many businesses and records, and yellow fever arrived for the first time in the summer and fall of 1878. Approximately 300 people perished from the disease. Constant caving caused the riverbank at Greenville to become unstable, and it was not uncommon for people to pull their businesses and homes away from the river's edge. In March 1890, a crevasse at Huntington and Catfish Points in Bolivar County emptied the Mississippi River floodwaters into the town. In just seven short years, another flood covered the north end of town. Again, in 1903 the levee broke south of the town and water backed into Greenville. The east side of the county experienced flooding in 1912. The long-suffering residents of Washington County underwent numerous trials.

In spite of the hardships in the region, improvements were many. The Mississippi Levee Board strengthened the levees. The Delta's first railroad, finished just before the yellow fever epidemic of 1878, ran from Greenville to Stoneville on Deer Creek, a distance of 10 miles. In the mid-1880s, a second railroad ran the length of the Delta from New Orleans to Memphis, crossing the first railroad at Elizabeth, east of Stoneville. At the turn of the century, Greenville was becoming a city. There was a diverse population that included Jews, Italians, and Chinese. The town had an electric streetcar line, and new permanent brick building were being erected. Schools, with Mr. E.E. Bass at the helm, were progressive. The names of private social clubs like Elysian, Olympian, Knights of Pythia, and Elks were often in the newspaper for their dances, dinners, and parades. President Teddy Roosevelt even came to bear hunt with some of his Washington County friends.

Washington County became economically strong. The lumber industry blossomed, and many short lines of railroad were constructed to take the trees to the mills. The county at one time had more concrete highways than any other county in the state. Washington County, no longer isolated, was on its way to becoming the richest area of the state.

On April 21, 1927, the most disastrous and costly break in the levees occurred in the Mound Landing levee, 15 miles north of Greenville. All of Washington County and the southern end of the Delta to the Yazoo River 100 miles away were under water until June. Washington County was again forced to rebuild its economic base from crops to railroads.

The recovery from the flood took place during the years of the Great Depression. The high points of the decade included the mechanization of farm equipment, the cutoffs of the river bends, the construction of the Mississippi River Bridge and the Greenville Air Base, and the establishment of the Delta Branch Experiment Station.

Washington County has produced more writers per capita than any other county in the United States. Among the most well-known authors from Washington County are Carrie Stern, William Alexander Percy, David L. Cohn, Walker Percy, Shelby Foote, Ellen Douglas, Bern Keating, Hodding Carter, Brooks Haxton, Kenneth Haxton, Dave Berry, Angela Jackson, and Clifton Taulbert. Jim Henson, the creator of the Muppets, was born in Greenville and spent his youth in Leland. The county also celebrates famous hometown heroes in blues music, scientific research, and the towing industry.

One

ANTEBELLUM

Karl Bodmer, a Swiss watercolorist, traveled down the Mississippi River in the late 1820s and painted this view of New Mexico, Washington County's first county seat. Bodmer vaguely recorded its location as "below the mouth of the Arkansas River." Although no definite location has been determined, many believe the town to have been located near present-day Mayersville in Issaquena County. (Joslyn Museum.)

Dr. Stephen Duncan of Natchez was once the largest slave owner in Mississippi and one of only five men to own more than 1,000 slaves in the entire South. Duncan owned eight plantations and produced more than 4,000 bales of cotton annually on his Washington and Issaquena County properties. He also was the owner of two highly productive sugar plantations in Louisiana.

One of three original vaults still stands at Baleshed Landing on the Mississippi River. The vault, built in 1830 by Dr. Stephen Duncan, was used to house money and the records of the cotton sales made along the river.

Frederick G. Turnbull, one of Washington County's earliest settlers, built Esperanza Plantation and later sold it to his brother Andrew Turnbull. Colonel Ed Richardson later owned the home and sold it to Mr. T.B. Cowan. He gave the house and several thousand acres of rich Delta cotton land surrounding the old mansion to Mr. P.L. Mann.

A family poses for a photograph in the shade at the rear of Esperanza.

St. John's Church was built in 1856 on land donated by Jonathan McCaleb of Greenfield Plantation. Of English Gothic design and style, it was the third Episcopal church built in Mississippi. Jesse Crowell, a slave owned by Frederick G. Turnbull, supervised the cutting of timber and the lumber preparation for the doors, windows, and pews. He handcarved the leaves and ferns on the communion rail and altar. During the War between the States, the lead was stripped from the stained-glass widows to make bullets. With no windows in place, the Delta's humid weather took its toll on the ornate building. Attempts were made to restore the church's splendor, but a 1904 tornado ripped the roof off and dashed all hopes of repairing the building. Wade Hampton of Washington County, Mississippi and Columbia, South Carolina, a large planter, Civil War general governor, and U.S. senator from South Carolina, was a founder of this church.

In the 1890s, these St. John's Episcopal Church members at Glen Allan pose near one of the tombs.

Arriving early in 1828 from Scott County, Kentucky, Junius R. Ward, one of the earliest settlers in Washington County along with Frederick Turnbull, purchased a large tract of land at the head of Lake Washington in 1829. He ultimately owned 875 acres of prime land and had a family of nine children.

In 1829, Junius R. Ward built the Erwin House, the oldest house in Washington County. His father, William Ward, served as the Choctaw Indian agent for the U.S. government. The original log-cabin features of the house can still be seen inside the home. Owned today by Mrs. Margaret Erwin Shutt, the Erwin House has been in the possession of Ward's descendants since it was constructed. The house was placed on the National Register of Historic Places in 1975.

Wade Hampton III was the epitome of the aristocratic Southern plantation owner and a scion of one of the South's wealthiest families. Coming to southern Washington County in 1844, Hampton purchased five plantations—Wild Woods, Richland, Otterbourne, Bayou Place, and Bear Garden. These holdings consisted of 10,253 acres and were attended by 900 servants. Hampton made his home at Wild Woods, a Louisiana-style elevated cottage. He also constructed a horse race track at the rear of his home. He stayed on his Mississippi properties part of the year, while the rest of his time was spent in South Carolina. He was a noted general in the War between the States and equipped, at his own expense, a regiment known as Hampton's Legion. After the war, Hampton was elected governor of South Carolina and later served as a senator and a railroad commissioner. Wade Hampton III was a successful Washington County planter for 58 years.

Born in 1841 in Columbia, South Carolina, Maj. Wade Hampton IV served the South in the War between the States. After the war, he married and moved to his father's plantation, Wild Woods, where he became a planter. He died of malaria in 1879 at Wild Woods.

Peru was one of the plantations in the Lake Washington area owned by Col. Ed Richardson, the largest cotton planter in the world in the 1870s and 1880s. Pictured here in the 1880s are the farm laborers, house, and steam gin.

Surrounded by several thousands of acres of land, Everhope was built in the 1830s by Andrew Knox, a planter from South Carolina. This home stood on the northwestern edge of Lake Washington and was later owned by Buddy McKamy and his family. A fire in 1992 destroyed Everhope.

Andrew Knox of South Carolina was the original owner of Solitaire Plantation, located west of Lake Washington, and the Knox family members are buried in the family cemetery on the place. On the grounds of Solitaire, drilling for oil occurred three different times, the first in 1927. The flood of 1927 "froze" the drill stem and bit in the hole. During the second attempt in 1929, drillers struck salt water that had natural gas in it. The last try occurred in 1931, when a tornado blew down the derrick. The main house, shown here covered by snow in the winter of 1939, burned in 1952.

Mrs. Sarah Prince, who, after her husband died, married John Miller, a wealthy planter who died in 1874, built Berkley Plantation in 1832. Mrs. Miller died in 1846 and was buried in Natchez. Mr. Miller had ordered in his will that he be buried in New Orleans and that his wife be buried next to him. Upon his death, when the riverboat passed Natchez, the family stopped and removed Mrs. Miller's remains from the vault and took both of them to St. Louis Cemetery.

Mount Holly was built in 1856 at Chatham on Lake Washington for Margaret Johnson Erwin, the daughter of early planter Henry Johnson of Kentucky. This 30-room mansion hosted numerous dignitaries, including Henry Clay and Samuel Sloan, a noted builder and possibly the designer of Mount Holly.

18

Sidney I. Law built the Law house at Foote in 1902. Mr. Law ordered this house from Sears & Roebuck Company. When he finished putting the house together, he realized that he was one board short. When he found it on a tenant's house on the place, he thought they needed it more than he did and left it there.

Linden Plantation was the site of one of the earliest settlements in Washington County, that of Frederick G. Turnbull in 1825. Turnbull built the first home in the county and named it Linden. Later this property belonged to Christopher F. Hampton, who built the second Linden house. In 1914, Mr. P.L. Mann built the present Linden, which is located on Lake Washington. Linden was placed on the National Register of Historic Places in 1982.

Frederick G. Turnbull, a land speculator and owner of a great deal of property, built Marathon Plantation in the late 1830s. This beautiful home was lost in a chess game to Turnbull's friend Albert Dunbar, an early scientist. Turnbull and Dunbar played the game from their homes by sending a slave on horseback back and forth with written messages showing their moves on the chessboard. Rob Roy Fisher and his family later made Marathon their home, and Fisher became a very successful planter.

This rear view of the Marathon house shows the barn, dovecote, cotton gin, mule sheds, and wagon barns. Situated at one time on the railroad, Marathon is today located on Highway 1, east of Lake Washington.

Longwood, built on land purchased by Ben Smith of Kentucky for 25¢ per acre, was constructed in 1832. Smith eventually purchased numerous other properties, totaling 30,000 acres. Although hit by a tornado, part of the original home still stands at Longwood and is encompassed by cotton fields.

Completed in 1859, Belmont at Wayside was constructed of bricks made on the plantation. It was originally the home of the Dr. William W. Worthington family, which included six children. The Union Army visited the home several times during the War between the States, during which the troops plundered cotton, mules, cows, hogs, food, and personal items from the Worthingtons. Belmont is one of only a few antebellum structures still standing in Washington County. (WAP.)

In 1845, Alexander B. Montgomery built Swiftwater, a Louisiana-style plantation home. Red brick piers were matched to the red roof of this home, while gallery porches were featured on three sides. Full-length windows helped keep the home cool. Mr. Montgomery, the brother of William Pinckney Montgomery, sold this home to Col. Ed Richardson, and he and his family moved to Texas.

Samuel Worthington built this large, imposing residence as the center of his 4,000-acre plantation. It was constructed in the early 1830s entirely of readily available cypress lumber and had at least 20 rooms. The cost for the home was reported to have been $35,000, including the furniture. Samuel Worthington, one of four brothers, was one of the most successful planters in Washington County. This fine old home stood for 100 years but was destroyed by levee construction in the 1930s.

Thomas Worthington, born in 1855 on Leota Plantation, was the youngest child of Isaac Worthington, the first member of the family to settle in what is now the southern portion of Washington County. The four Worthington brothers, of whom Isaac was one, came from Kentucky during the 1830s. By the time of the War between the States, the brothers Samuel, William, Isaac, and Elisha had become very wealthy planters. Samuel graduated from the University of the South in Sewanee, Tennessee in 1877. He was a master Mason and a member of the Knights of Pythia. He also held membership with the Elks Club. He was elected in 1885 as a member of the board of supervisors, and in 1908, he became sheriff and tax collector.

During the antebellum period, William Alexander Percy (Gray Eagle) lived on the Percy Plantation located immediately across Deer Creek from Three Oaks. In the War between the States, Percy led the Swamp Guards Cavalry Company from Washington County. He would subsequently play a major role in county politics during the era of Reconstruction.

The Washington County seat of New Mexico was succeeded by Princeton, near Lake Washington, in 1830, and by Old Greenville in 1847. Old Greenville was then little more than a port on Bachelor's Bend for the hinterland and Deer Creek. Island 83, a large and well-farmed island sat in front of the town. Bacon Chute allowed access to the river. (WAP.)

Two

WAR BETWEEN THE STATES AND REBUILDING

Confederate guerrillas attacked passing boats from the Greenville Bends. As a result, the town's position on the river made it a target for passing gunboats. In 1863, Sherman dispatched steamers and men from his army at Vicksburg to take what they needed in supplies, stores, and beasts. Worried about Confederate troops crossing the river in the area, a patrol of the bends was in effect through 1864. The *Benton* was one of the patrol boats. (OCM.)

The Erin Guard of Washington County, as the name implies, had many Irishmen in its ranks. Captain William Hunt and William P. Montgomery largely organized it for their sons, Capt. George B. Hunt and Lt. John Malcolm Montgomery (pictured here). Montgomery resigned his commission and returned to Washington County. Later he joined the Bolivar Troops, Company H, 1st Mississippi Cavalry, along with his brother Dr. D.C. Montgomery. (PWN.)

Martin Marble, a slave of Washington County sheriff Andrew Carson, was credited with saving county records when Federal troops burned Old Greenville during the War between the States. He loaded the records in a wagon and hid in the swamps until the Yankees had left. Unlike many Southern counties, Washington County's records are very complete thanks to Marble's efforts.

Harriet Blanton Theobald earned the sobriquet "Mother of Greenville" for donating part of her Blantonia Plantation after the War between the States for the rebuilding of New Greenville. The present-day site is located a mile north of Old Greenville. (BK.)

Charles P. Huntington was president of the Greenville Construction Company and was responsible for building what is now the Columbus & Greenville Railroad. Huntington also donated a collection of books to Greenville in 1878 that became the basis for the city's first library. The library built to house the collection was located on the north side of Main Street, west of Walnut, and adjoining the Blanton-Theobald private cemetery. (WAP.)

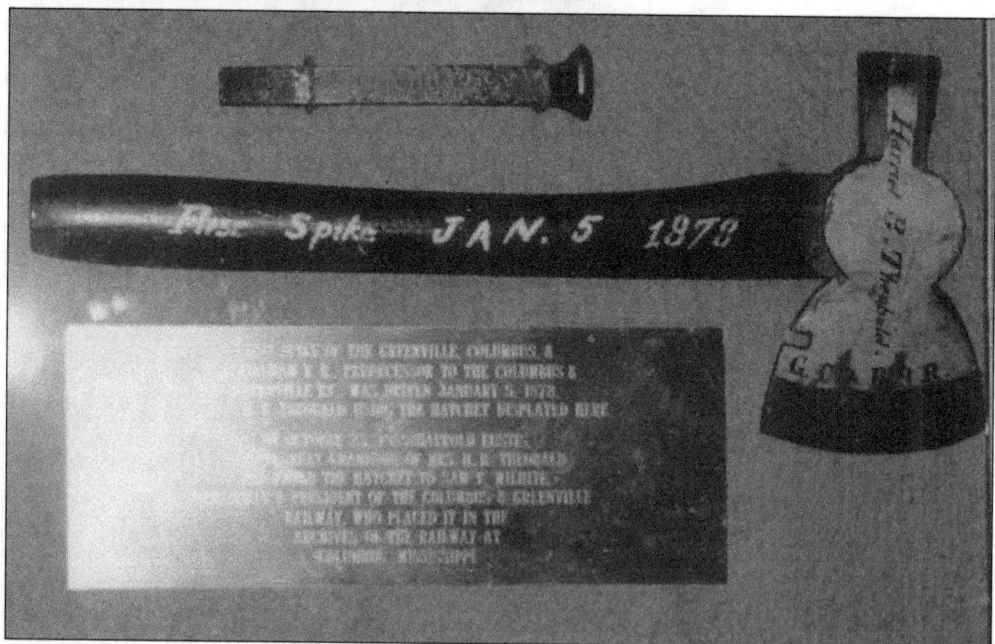

The first railroad in the Delta, the Greenville, Columbus & Birmingham Railroad, began in Greenville and ran east for 10 miles to Stoneville. Harriett B. Theobald drove the first spike with this hatchet on January 5, 1878. The line grew eastward and became the predecessor to the Columbus & Greenville Railway. (KN.)

The Swiftwater store on Swiftwater Plantation a few miles south of Greenville was built and owned by Ed Richardson. The platform near the tracks was used to ease the unloading of the trains. All the local planters in the Swiftwater area depended on this establishment for their supplies.

Beginning in August 1878, the names of yellow fever victims appeared in the Greenville newspaper with unnerving regularity. This issue contains two and a half columns of names of people who had died since the last issue. Unfortunately, many people did not realize that cisterns were a prime breeding places for the *Aedes aegypti* mosquito, the carrier of yellow fever. Greenville experienced 300 deaths in the epidemic of 1878. (PWN.)

The Greenfield Store, built by Ed Richardson in 1879, was located just below Glen Allan and supplied all the early planters and families before the town of Glen Allan had stores. The Greenfield Store was large and stocked groceries, hardware, clothing, and a full line of plantation supplies.

Old Chatham Store

The Stein family owned the Burn Plantation at the north end of Lake Washington, and their old store was a landmark for the Chatham area. The site of the original town of Chatham can be seen among the handful of buildings still in existence.

Alhambra Plantation, west of Lake Washington, is one of three plantations that carry a Spanish name in that area.

Duncansby, once a thriving town, suffered a fatal blow from a levee break in 1890. When the levee was rebuilt to the east, the town became extinct. Today the site of the old town is in Issaquena County. W.H. Brown Sr., a leading citizen of the town, had a plantation nearby.

The practice of clearing "new ground" became even more pronounced in the latter quarter of the 19th century. It was not uncommon for a planter to buy tree-laden land and sell the timber from it to a local sawmill or logging company to help offset the cost of purchasing the land. Small sawmills and large lumber companies from Ohio, Kentucky, and Indiana were at work around the county. (MP.)

Loggers cut the timber and brought their logs to the river. Great log rafts were lashed together and floated to sawmills downriver. (WAP.)

The Moseley family home, Bluella, was near Overby station, south of Hollandale and above Percy. A second story was added to the house in 1919. The gazebo/playhouse (not pictured), built before the house was remodeled, still stands in the yard. (DN.)

William Owsley Aldridge moved to Arcola in 1867 and, after college, began work for Dr. John Atterbury in 1877. By 1906, Aldridge owned Mulberry, Ditchley, Alma, and Wilmot Plantations. (LHF.)

William Beauregard Swain came to the Delta in 1880 and represented the new planter who reestablished the plantation system after the War between the States. His father, Samuel Swain, bought Hollyknowe and Dunleith Plantations with W.W. Stone. By the early 20th century, W.B. Swain also owned Fairfax, Randolph, Bamboo, and part of Paxton Plantations. (LHF.)

A Hollyknowe Plantation house for the Swain family was built as early as 1880 on Bogue Phalia. Just after the turn of the century, this structure was erected; it was later renovated during the prosperity of the 1920s into the current home. (KS.)

Christopher F. Hampton was called "Kit" by both his friends and family. Born in 1821 on Millwood Plantation near Columbia, South Carolina, he was the son of Wade Hampton II and Ann Fitzsimons. He built the second Linden Plantation home, after tearing down the original home for the construction of his new mansion. Hampton had purchased the Linden property, along with 10,000 acres, from Fredrick Turnbull, a land speculator and planter, in 1847. Kit was very successful in his agricultural pursuits and also owned several plantations in Issaquena County. He was known as a crack shot and an excellent horseman but also loved society. A gentle, retiring, and modest man, Kit Hampton died at Linden in 1886.

Col. Ed Richardson, the largest cotton planter in the world in the 1870s and 1880s, was the owner of 50 cotton plantations from Clarksdale to Yazoo City in Mississippi, including Refuge, Swiftwater, Esperanza, and Peru Plantations in Washington County, numerous plantations in Louisiana, and several more in Texas. He produced 15,000 bales annually for the market from his own plantations and was the owner of the largest cotton firm in New Orleans, known as Richardson and May, which handled over 112,000 bales per year. Richardson also owned numerous plantation supply stores on both sides of the Mississippi River. In addition, he purchased the Vicksburg, Shreveport & Pacific Railroad, and he bought the Wesson Cotton Mill in Wesson, Mississippi. He owned a very large home in Jackson, Mississippi and a mansion on St. Charles Street in New Orleans. He was also the chairman of the board for numerous banks in Mississippi and Louisiana. The *Ed Richardson* steamboat of New Orleans was named for him. His income was reported to be $500,000 per year. The convicts he used in his railroad and levee construction operations were leased to him by Mississippi. Richardson, in turn, used these for his plantation labor, which gave him the manpower needed to maintain his land and holdings. He also formed a partnership with Gen. N.B. Forrest and Gen. Wade Hampton in his leasing and cultivating of cotton on their plantations after the war. Subsequently, he bought both of these plantations from the generals.

The Tribbett gin, like the rail line of the same name, known as the Black Dog, are reminders of the connection between the railroads laid through the Delta in the 1880s. The Black Dog served Hollyknowe, Tribbett, Bourbon, Greenland, Trail Lake, and ended at Yerger or Darlove. (PWN.)

In the spring of 1898, the *Belle of the Bends* steamboat ran her first trip to Greenville. In the fall of that year, Greenville merchants presented the boat a silver water cooler. The boat offered moonlight excursions, and for more than a decade, on Tuesdays and Thursdays the boat left Greenville on its regular mail run to Vicksburg and way landings. It became the last side-wheeler in the packet trade to ply the waters below Memphis. (WAP.)

The Greenville Cotton Company illustrates the growing importance of Greenville as a center of cotton trade in the latter half of the 19th century.

The Greenville Ice and Coal Company, established in 1888, provided a necessary commodity for Greenville citizens during the winter and the notoriously hot summer months. (WAP.)

Major fires occurred in Greenville in 1874, in Leland in 1889, in Burdette in 1895, and in Leota and Arcola in 1900. Both Greenville and Leland rebuilt the business sections of their towns with brick. In February 1901, the Greenville volunteer fire department resigned and resolutions were passed for the creation of a fire company. By 1904, Chief E.V. Donovan announced that every engine would have a chemical apparatus and a fine team of bay horses. (WAP.)

Note the name Archer above the door in this brick schoolhouse located on the corner of Shelby and Johnson Streets in Greenville. It is said to be one of the first brick schools built in Mississippi. Later, the American Legion Stadium occupied this spot. (WAP.)

The first Jewish Temple in Greenville occupied the corner of Walnut and Main. In 1886, the Hebrew Assembly Hall, named for the Alexander family, was used as the schoolhouse. The boys met in the hall and the girls in the synagogue schoolrooms. The building was later moved to Campbell Street where it was divided into two residences. (WAP.)

The Bell Telephone Company came to Greenville in 1881. Deputy Noy Hunt lived in the rooms on the west side of the jail at the corner of Nelson Street, and his office was on the east side of the same building. Telephone #1 was in the hall between. Local educator Susie P. Trigg claims to have been the first to call "central." (WAP.)

The only known extant photograph of the Duncansby community was taken during the 1890 flood. The levee break at the town led to its extinction when a new levee was built to the east, throwing the town to the exposure of the river. The town was named for Dr. Stephen Duncan who once owned land in Washington County.

Among the people in the unique wooden boats, called bateau, at the Trigg House on Davis Street at the west end of Alexander are Judge and Mrs. W.R. Trigg and Eleanor Somerville. One significant result of the 1890 levee break at Huntington and Catfish Point was the decision to move back the levees on Catfish Point to allow more water to pass through the previously constricted area of the Mississippi River. (WAP.)

"Let us pray." Grand Master John M. Ware and William Cross laid the cornerstone for the Washington County Courthouse in 1891. John F. Barnes was the builder, the McDonald Brothers the architects, and L.T. Thomas the mason. In the background stands the jail. (WAP.)

While the protection levee kept downtown Greenville dry in the flood of 1897, the courthouse and jail grounds east of the railroad tracks went under water. After this flood, the government built a set back levee known as the Huntington Short Line, resulting in 14 plantations being left to the river. The beginning point of this levee was at Mound Landing where caving was already rapidly occurring. (WAP.)

The Elysian Club represents one of the many social clubs in Greenville at the turn of the century. Most of them did not have a permanent meeting place and therefore met in the upper rooms of a building on the corner of Walnut and Main Streets. Beginning in 1900, new homes were built for the social clubs, and the Elysians moved into their home on the corner of Main and Shelby. Later the Elysian Club became the site of the William Alexander Percy Memorial Library. (WAP.)

The new Grand Opera House in Greenville, completed in mid-April 1900, stood on the corner of Main and Poplar where the Federal Building stands today. George H. Johnston of St. Louis, a scenic artist and decorator, painted scenery and the decorations. John F. Barnes, a Greenville contractor, put on the final touches. Since Jim Crow laws were in effect at the time, the upper half of the balcony was reserved for African Americans. (WAP.)

Three

A New Century

The Greenville front was paved in the second decade of the 20th century. Across the river from Greenville, a government fleet had a permanent station. At the turn of the century, diesel-powered boats began to compete with the steamboats. Both of these types of boat had competition from the growing web of rail lines. (WAP.)

The second railroad in the Delta, the Louisville, New Orleans & Texas, was completed in 1885 and transversed the Delta from New Orleans to Memphis. A loop line from Wilczinski (Metcalfe) to Hampton and later Rolling Fork included Greenville and Wayside. At that time, a ticket to Greenville cost 50¢ for the Fourth of July excursion train. (WAP.)

Napanee, and Dunkirk (above) were on a dummy line (a short railroad with no turn around), north of Elizabeth. Many of these dummy lines were built through the uncleared Delta to allow loggers access to transportation of their logs. (MP.)

Marlowe Park Jr., at Dunkirk, watches while his father and a gypsy trade a mule for his new pony, Dixie. Park compared the transaction to the modern equivalent of trading a work truck for a four-wheeler. (MP.)

Sharecropper's homes were a great contrast to the lifestyle of the plantation owner. Sharecroppers farmed small plots of land for a share of the crop's profits. Their small homes had a garden and pens for cows, chickens, and turkeys. They were often given a mule to work the crop. (PWN.)

Plantation hands lived in simple homes. The residents of this house sit behind a quilt for shade. Such homes were called "shotgun houses" because the rooms are lined up one after the other so that one could shoot a shotgun through the front door and out the back. At the far left is the outhouse, or privy. These homes have disappeared since the Civil Rights Movement of the 1960s. (PWN.)

It is time for work, and two mules are hitched to each plow in this early morning scene near Murphy. (DN.)

Large gangs of mules were sent across the fields in long lines on a plantation. This was the equivalency of the modern-day jumbo tractors.

Aside from the cash crops, it was necessary to grow corn and crops to feed the mules that were necessary for working the farms. A man is riding the plow while another rides a mule to direct the team of eight mules. (MP.)

Before the days of mechanization, field hands were used to maintain crops by removing unwanted weeds with hoes. After World War II, the country became more industrialized, and many of the hands moved north seeking a different style of life. Farmers began to use herbicides and pesticides to control the growth of weeds. (WP.)

Cotton pickers line up to pick a large Delta cotton field near Glen Allan.

Cotton pickers load cotton into large cane baskets on Peru Plantation.

In 1933, the government ordered farmers to plow up their knee-high cotton in order to boost the low prices caused by the Depression. An example of the actual work is recorded here on the Weilenman farm near Stoneville. (BW.)

The scale often located on the turn row in the field illustrates one method of weighing cotton here; hand-picked cotton was placed in suspended woven baskets to be weighed. (WAP.)

The scale and companion "pea" were used to weigh hand-picked cotton in the sack at the field. The 6- or 9-foot sacks were raised on a long pole above the trailers and emptied. A good worker could pick 300 pounds of cotton a day and might be paid as high as $1 per hundred pounds. (WP.)

Here is a steam-powered gin located near Glen Allan in 1912.

Mr. J.M. Jefferies built this gin on Wild Woods plantation, the former plantation of Wade Hampton III.

The Greenville Compress on the Old Leland Road held many bales of cotton before they were shipped to mills. The rail line can be seen entering from the back. (GC.)

The Greenville Compress used this compress for many years. They purchased the machine in New Orleans in 1917. (GC.)

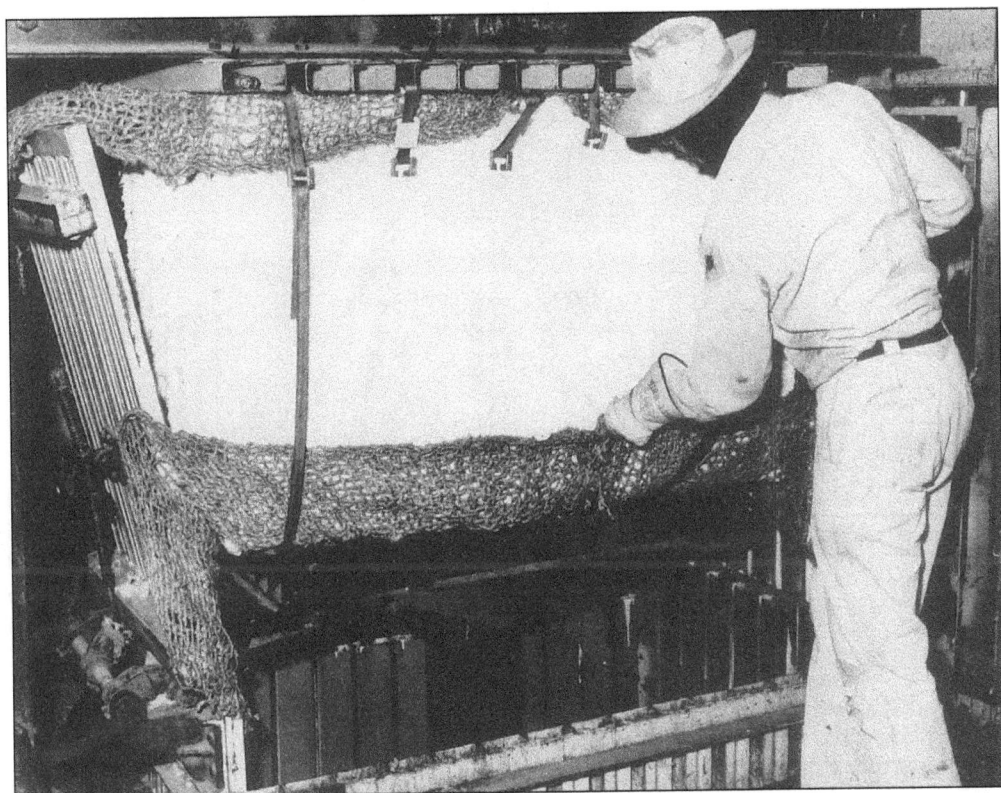

Compressing ginned cotton into a bale weighing around 500 pounds is done in a matter of minutes. Burlap bagging is placed above and below the unstrapped bale, and the compressor shapes the bale. While the bale is compressed, metal straps are fastened and secured. (GC.)

Rail and barge were the original form of transportation used for shipping bales of cotton to the cotton mills. Today large trucks do the hauling. (DBES.)

Charles Berry, the inventor of the one-row Gamble-Berry cotton picker, tried out his mechanical picker in Washington County with much success. As in other well-known cases, his invention was copied and patented by a large equipment company. (WAP.)

Experimental cotton pickers came in many forms. Modern cotton practices have found that cotton yields more when planted with skip rows between every four rows. The biggest pickers today are made to fit this planting style. Today's cotton picker has amenities such as radios and air-conditioned cabs. Cotton has been genetically bred to grow only to a certain height to make better use of the mechanical cotton picker. (WAP.)

During the days of mule power a spray rig for boll weevil and other pests consisted of a man on a mule patting sacks of dust. In the middle of the last century, Willie Ray Smith, an entomologist, experimented with a hand-held insect duster at the Delta Branch Experiment Station in Stoneville. (WAP.)

The Delta Branch Experiment Station in Stoneville began in 1904 and has made many achievements in scientific agricultural research. The Stoneville Duster is an example of one of the experimental pieces of equipment used on the station.

The McGee Dean store owned by B.O. McGee and Charles Dean served Leland and the surrounding country. The store was on Main Street across from the old depot and continued to operate until after World War II. In this picture, Sanford McGee is seated to the right of his son Clyde McGee (in bow tie and hat). (DOB.)

The largest store in Glen Allan was this store, built in 1918 and owned by Mr. C.G. Youngblood. It was 50 feet by 80 feet in size and carried the best materials available, as well as a very large selection of plantation supplies. Youngblood lived with his family in the top half of this store. (DOB.)

Joel Slater Myers and his daughter Katherine Myers (Mrs. John Pearson) pose with their plantation workers at Baleshead. Dr. Stephen Duncan owned this plantation from 1830 to 1860.

The B.B. Payne store in Winterville, shown in this 1917 photograph, sold shoes, ribbon, lace, and sundry dry goods. It later became Mrs. Watt's store and post office. Although once a commercial center for isolated plantation dwellers and a rural population burdened with poor travel conditions, stores like this have given way to urban malls. This building was demolished in 1999. (GTC.)

Towns swelled in population on "Ration Day." The workhands of McGee and Dean have come to Leland to receive their monthly rations and supplies. The men on horses are in front of the old Bank of Leland on the corner of Third and Broad Streets. (DOB.)

In its earliest days, the Delta was well known for its artesian, or free-flowing, wells and its underlying, copious aquifer that produced a water table nearing the land's surface. However, a larger population and increased water usage by farmers in rice fields and catfish ponds have required officials to regulate these wells. (MP.)

Cisterns were used to collect rainwater most often via a system of pipes that carried the rain from the roof of the house. The crank pump was connected to a belt of small buckets, which emptied into the nozzle and provided water to wash clothes and for general household use. (GTC.)

Washington County receives 52 inches of rain annually and is well known for its beautiful ox bow lakes formed by abandoned bends of the river. These lakes are often used for baptisms by small country churches.

Pictured from left to right, Jeff Wilkerson, three of his Payne cousins—Billy, Tom, and Hugh (Tut)—and a workhand show off the results of a rabbit hunt. During this time, rabbits were plentiful, but deer were scarce in the Mississippi Delta. Hunting deer was not revived until the population was restocked in the 1940s. (PWN.)

Metcalfe, occupying a small strip of land between Black Bayou and Deer Creek, was called Wilczinski until 1910. A "Y" in the railroad juncture allowed a loop line of railroad to come to Greenville, giving the town access to Memphis and New Orleans by rail. In the autumn, "hog killings" provided ham, bacon, and hocks for the winter for the people on Shamrock Plantation, located near Metcalfe. (RO.)

In 1913, Greenville had four hose companies. The department had three combination hose wagons, one combination truck company, and 18 members. A new two-story brick firehouse was built on Washington Avenue, between Harvey Street and the depot. (WAP.)

In February 1904, the Hollandale fire bell rang on the corner of Washington Street. Lost in the fire were the Masonic Hall, McGhee's General Merchandise, Golden & McAlpin Grocery, the post office, the Collum Hotel and livery, Rubenstein Dry Goods, Cousinan Grocery, Holland & Hays General Merchandise, Tucker & Peters, Crouch's Grocery, the McAlpine Hotel, Dr. Magruder's office, and Spivey & Magruder's. (WAP.)

DUMPING 1907

The building, repairing, raising, and maintaining of the levees that prevent breaks (crevasses) and overflows (floods) were a perpetual fact of life. In the absence of modern machinery, mules, dirt scrapers, and workers were the three essentials for the manual levee work. The work was seasonal, and it was common for weather, high water in the river, the quarantines necessitated by the threat of yellow fever, or the priority of the harvest to hamper levee maintenance. (WAP.)

In 1903, a crevasse formed south of Greenville. The water backed into town, though it did not cover the downtown area. These refugees paddle near the corner of Poplar and Main Street. In the center, the wagon pulled by mules is above the floodwater. (WAP.)

Manual labor was used to dig the ditches for the sewer system. By the end of August 1901, practically the entire city was covered by the sewer system, except for Broadway from Vallient to Deaton. Once the system was in place street paving could begin. The town's sewer system emptied into the Mississippi River near the town dump. (WAP.)

Greenville's first paved streets, Washington Avenue and Walnut Street between the depots, a distance of 4,300 feet, were laid in 1902. Main Street between Walnut and Shelby, at 1,050 feet, was finished next, and finally Poplar Street between Main and Washington completed a block, which totaled 6,350 feet, more than 1 mile. Note the Methodist Church in the background, as well as the mounds of bricks that would be used to complete the paving after streetcar rails were placed. (WAP.)

Mr. and Mrs. N.V. Richardson ran the Washington County poorhouse from 1946 to 1948 and then Mr. Richardson went to work as a deputy sheriff serving under three different sheriffs. Mr. Richardson also ran the first streetcar in Greenville in the early 1900s.

In 1909, a site was selected for the Delta Fairgrounds and a city park with streetcar service. Of the 42 acres chosen, 15 were for the park and 2 belonged to the Country Club. The park had a race track, a baseball diamond, stalls, refreshment booths, a bandstand, a dancing pavilion, and swings. The debt-ridden Delta Fairgrounds only lasted until 1912. That year, Bolivar County refugees were taken to the grounds.

The dance pavilion at Greenway Park, built by J.W. Bermingham, was completed in the fall of 1909. The expansion, which was completed shortly thereafter, included the covering of the bandstand (built earlier in the summer), the addition of seats around the edge, and the construction of a platform for the band dressing rooms. The roof projected out so far that it precluded the possibility of a dance being ruined by rain.

Pictured here is the Leader baseball team at Greenway Park. From left to right are (front row) Eddie Copeland, Charlie Cadenhead, Naddie McBride, Witty Griffin, and Terry Massey; (back row, in no particular order) an unidentified player, R.K. Haxton, Otto Wineman, Paul Pierce, Virgil Payne, Alec Ransom, and Joe Wall. (WAP.)

The Greenville Country Club bought 2 acres adjacent to the Delta Fairgrounds in 1909. The original clubhouse faced the race track and was built high enough so that members could stand on the gallery and watch the races. Tennis courts were also erected at an early date. Over the years other clubhouses were built, but today the Buster Brown Community Center (built in the 1930s) is the only remaining clubhouse of that era. (DBES.)

Paul L. Mann came to Glen Allan in 1888 as a 19-year-old clerk for Mr. T.B. Cowan. His salary was $25 per month, and he was given room and board. Mr. Mann later inherited five plantations, interest in a hotel, a bank, railroad stock, several commissary stores, and a lot of cash from his employer, Mr. Cowan. With nearly 5,800 acres of land, Mr. Mann decided to sell part of his holdings. He later moved from his Esperanza plantation to Glen Allan where he purchased Linden Plantation. He tore the old Linden house down and, in 1914, built his new Linden home, the most beautiful home on Lake Washington. It was fully staffed with a cook, a chauffeur, a yard boy, a butler, a groom, and several maids. Mr. Mann was the wealthiest man in this community.

Architect H. Walters was contracted to build the Cowan Hotel, a 3-story, 70-room hotel, which was equipped with elevators and steam heat. At a special ceremony on March 2, 1901, Mrs. N.P. Hawkins, George Wheatley, J.F. Negus, James Robertshaw, and Henry T. Ireys laid the first bricks. James G. Smith took charge at the opening on March 18, 1902, while Bob Halett waited on customers in his barbershop downstairs. Later a fourth floor and extension were added. (WAP.)

In the lobby of the Cowan Hotel guests could find a good selection of cigars. At its peak, the hotel had 100 telephones. The Cowan held the insurance office of John Hebron and a restaurant, among other businesses. (WAP.)

Born a slave, Holt Collier, a famous bear hunter, later served in the Confederate army. He was chosen as the guide for President Teddy Roosevelt's bear hunt.

President Theodore Roosevelt enjoyed bear hunting in the Delta. He often went to the woods with his friends from Washington County: (1) Dr. Ricey, (2) Harley Metcalfe, (3) Theodore Roosevelt, and (4) Clive Metcalfe. At this time the bear was disappearing in the Delta. Roosevelt refused to shoot a captured bear, and the story of this hunt grew. As a result, the teddy bear toy was created, and it became very popular with children. (WAP.)

All boys are lined up by height in front of the Leland school. The girls entered the school separately. (BW.)

In 1888, the Catholic Church held a strawberry festival to raise money for a schoolhouse. St. Rose of Lima on the corner of Main and Hines had 19 rooms, including a kitchen and dining room. This original house was destroyed by fire and was soon rebuilt. (WAP.)

Jewish families first came to Washington County after the War between the States. Among the first to arrive were merchants Morris Weiss and Nathan Goldstein, who established a business in 1870. In addition to commerce, Jewish leaders Jacob Alexander, Theodore Pohl, and the Wilczinski brothers were involved in every part of community life. The Hebrew Union of Greenville was chartered on November 28, 1880. Grand Master Charles Blum laid the cornerstone of the current temple in March 1906. (WAP.)

Built in Blanton Park in 1907, the three-story Elks Home was constructed with a "double deck" stone-pillared gallery, the pillars capped by terra cotta stone pieces. Note in the center under the peak of the roof is a large gilded elk's head. A bowling alley, a gymnasium, and a barbershop were located in the basement. Upstairs rooms included a billiard room, a ladies parlor, an observatory, and a reading room. (WAP.)

Central School faced Central Street near Theobald. (WAP.)

Mrs. Harriet Blanton Theobald donated the southwest corner of her residence block, known as Blanton Park, to the Methodist Church. The first brick was laid for the new church building in the spring of 1900. By 1904 there were three buildings on the block facing Washington Avenue—the Methodist Church, Dr. Odeneal's Sanitarium, and the Elks Club. (WAP.)

In 1905 the Baptists moved their church site from Poplar Street to the present-day location on Main Street. By the turn of the century, Greenville was no longer a city of old wooden churches. (WAP.)

When the new church was completed in 1887, St. James Episcopal Church was moved from its central location near Main and Walnut to an area considered to be in the "country" at the corner of Washington Avenue and Broadway. Remodeling of the building allowed it to accommodate the growing congregation. A brick veneer was added to the church in 1919. (WAP.)

The present site of St. Joseph's Roman Catholic Church on Main and Shelby was purchased in 1874. Father Korstenbroeck was named pastor in 1886 and remained until 1920. Father Korstenbroeck, who had studied architecture before entering the priesthood in Holland, designed the church that was built in 1906. (WAP.)

Catholic Church, Greenville, Miss.

Sacred Heart Roman Catholic Church of the Divine Word began as a school for African-American youths in 1913. It was also the site of St. Augustine Seminary, the first seminary for the training of African-American priests in the United States. The present Romanesque-style church was built in 1928. (WAP.)

The King's Daughters Circle purchased a home on the corner of Central and Theobald in the spring of 1897 for $900. It was a shotgun house made up of two bedrooms and a kitchen. It is seen here in the floodwaters of 1903. (WAP.)

In the fall of 1888 it was noted that the Greenville post office had electric lights. While the office was becoming more modern, the town needed to catch up. In 1899, a memo was sent from the U.S. Postal Service to Greenville announcing that if Greenville did not "mend [its] ways" by providing sidewalks in the free delivery district before October, service would be withdrawn. Construction began on a new post office in 1909. (WAP.)

Offering care since 1894, the King's Daughters operated from cottages before erecting a permanent hospital in 1905 with J.F. Barnes being awarded the building contract. The first baby born in the hospital was the son of Mr. and Mrs. W.B. Swain. The hospital, located on the corner of Arnold and Walker Streets, was razed in 1937 and replaced by the Mediterranean-style Bessie Taylor Home. (WAP.)

In July 1909 the Greenville Post Office became the first federal building to be constructed in the Delta. At the dedication, Pink Smith made an address on behalf of Postmistress Mrs. N.S. Neilson. A deed to the site and a Bible were included in the cornerstone, and the event was celebrated at the new park with a barbecue of beef, mutton, pork, and ham for 1,000 people. (WAP.)

77

Senator LeRoy Percy is a favorite son of Washington County and a man whose great leadership left a permanent mark on Greenville and the county. Percy opposed the Ku Klux Klan by speaking out against their intolerance. (BK.)

On Friday, January 11, 1901, the home of LeRoy and Camille Percy, the parents of William Alexander Percy, burned. Six months later a new foundation was laid on Broadway. (WAP.)

The Olympian Club members held a "shirt waist," or their first non-formal party, in 1900. The private Jewish social club met in the rooms of the Opera House in 1905. Their home on Washington Avenue, next door to the Elks, was completed in 1912. (WAP.)

The ladies in this car have decorated it with flowers from friends' gardens. Note the set of deer or elk antlers, indicating that they are representing the Elks Club in the parade. Goldie Ham, Bess Ham, Edna Bell Ham, and Mattye Lucy Crouch enjoy the ride. (WAP.)

In 1912 the levee broke at Hughes Landing near Beulah in Bolivar County, and the water moved south and east. Napanee Plantation north of Elizabeth was a place of great concern during the 1912 flood because a group of lumber men were stranded there for some time without supplies. The occupants of the Giddin house sit casually posed on the roof of their porch at mid-day. (DOB.)

The town of Athol sprung up in 1885, when the Louisville, New Orleans & Texas Railroad crossed the Georgia Pacific. The town later changed its name to Elizabeth. These two railroads represented the first railroad crossing in the Mississippi Delta. The 1912 flood covered Elizabeth's main street. (BW.)

W.B. Swain's Hollyknowe store sat facing the railroad track. Each plantation had a store that served as a post office and a center of activity for the community. (DOB.)

The 1912 flood continued south from Elizabeth to Leland, Dunleith, Hollyknowe, Tribette, Trail Lake, and Darlove. The water flowed into the Sunflower River, causing the river to rise and to flood Indianola. Refugees such as these at Holly Knowe made camps on ridges. In the right background is the cooking area and the main house is in the left background. Clothes and bedding are hung on ropes wires and fences. (DOB.)

High water came again in 1913, and Greenville experienced another close call when a whirlpool created an unusual caving at the end of Washington Avenue. Half the levee gave way, and the willow mat revetment was washed away.

Spectators were drawn to the levee at Greenville to see the caving, caused by a whirlpool, that threatened their town. Nearby houses were immediately torn down and paid for later. From both sides, citizens watched the prisoners who worked on a causeway to repair the levee and to protect the town from crevasse. Using prison and farm labor, the repair was completed in a record 60 hours. (WAP.)

The first major hard-surfaced highway construction program for Washington County was approved in 1916. The laborers here load sand, gravel, and bagged cement into batches, which are dumped on the conveyor belt and deposited into the skip. Then the skip is raised, allowing the mix to fall into a rotating drum where water is added. When sufficiently mixed, the concrete is discharged from the back of the drum onto the prepared roadbed, smoothed, and allowed to harden. (WAP.)

C.C. Thornton, a stationmaster, stands across old Highway 1 (paved with concrete in 1918) from the B.B. Payne General Merchandise Store and post office in Winterville. Winterville was established on the original branch line of the Louisville, New Orleans & Texas Railroad (now the Illinois Central Railroad) built to Huntington and Arkansas City in 1885. (GTC.)

Washington County towns were historically sparse in population and did not require many peacekeepers, except on Saturday nights when the plantation labor overflowed the towns to shop. The rowdies often wound up in the calaboose, or jail. In 1899 Greenville built a new jail known affectionately as the "Hotel de Ville." In this photograph are Greenville policemen Bill Chipman (right) and Officer McClain (left), who served Greenville in the 1920s. Uniquely, Greenville employed African-American police officers as early as 1885. (WAP.)

Policemen with batons, dogs, and horses show off the new mechanized police force. (WAP.)

The center of the block on the west side of Walnut Street between Main and Washington was a division known as Wausau Court. At the base of the levee was the police headquarters. The 1927 flood refugees used the cars parked on the levee to dry their clothes and bedding. The station was removed when the levee was redirected in the 1930s. (WAP.)

Bootlegging was a common practice in Washington County in the 1920s despite national prohibition. Shown here displayed outside the jail are copper tubs and tubing, washtubs, funnels, jugs, and wooden barrels that have all been brought in with the capture of whiskey stills. (WAP.)

In the foreground the fence is in good condition, while in the distance it has fallen over. Guards walked the levee night and day during high water and reported any change or sign of danger to headquarters. At night the guards carried lanterns for illumination. This act gave the title to William Alexander Percy's famous autobiography, *Lanterns on the Levee*, about life in Washington County from the late 1800s to the mid-1900s. (WAP.)

The wooden "fence" built to protect the sandbags has given way and left the bags exposed to the wash of the water. Note, at the upper right, the farm headquarters and, at the far right, a barge with levee workers. (WAP.)

The last attempts to prevent overflow were the sandbags placed on top of the levees. The side of this levee is also covered with bags to prevent a sloughing levee. (WAP.)

During high water a sand boil could occur on the dry side of the levee. Clear water indicated little threat, but when sand and mud were in the water it usually meant the undermining of the levee. Sandbags were placed around the boil to prevent its growing larger or a break as in the sub-levee shown here. Sub-levees were small levees built outside the main levee. (WAP.)

A hand-posted sign shows the rising river stage at Greenville on the levee behind the Levee Board building in April 1927. Forty-two feet is considered flood stage on the Greenville gauge. Flood stage indicates the height that the river must reach to go over its banks and make levees necessary for control. (WAP.)

POSTAL TELEGRAPH – COMMERCIAL CABLES

CLARENCE H MACKAY, PRESIDENT

TELEGRAMS TO ALL AMERICA

CABLEGRAMS TO ALL THE WORLD

31MHA 11

GREENVILLE MISS APL 21 1927

J M HOWORTH

131   414 ½ EAST C APITOL ST JACKSON MISS

LEVEE BROKE NEAR SCOTT WATER MAY BE IN GREENVILLE BY NIGHT

LUCY SOMERVILLE

930A

This telegram says it all in one sentence. Married to J.M. Howorth the next year, Lucy Somerville served as a state legislator and in several federal positions under four U.S. presidents. In 1923, her mother, Nellie Nugent Somerville, became the first woman elected to the Mississippi State Legislature. (WAP.)

At Mound Landing, floodwaters rushed through the break with great force. The river emptied on to the farmland and washed across fences, roads, pastures, and newly planted crops. Wherever the water met an obstacle it used its force to continue along unchecked. (WAP.)

It took approximately 12 hours for the floodwaters to reach Greenville. During those hours, four trains left Greenville carrying approximately 2,000 people. The Columbus & Greenville attempted to take one more train out of Greenville near midnight. Two miles from town at Paducah, a flag stop near Fish Lake, the train was hit by a wave 2 to 3 feet high, which put out the train's fires. (WAP.)

In 1868 six former slaves established Mount Horeb Missionary Baptist Church, the first African-American church in Greenville. Originally located on Levee Street, it was moved to this location on the corner of Nelson and Broadway in 1909. This church was replaced in the 1970s. Many organizational meetings were held in the building to the right during the early days of the Civil Rights Movement. (WAP.)

In the 1927 flood, the waters crept into Greenville from the north and finally stood 6 to 8 feet deep in the church. (WAP.)

The floodwaters passed over Washington and Main Street and surrounded the Mississippi Levee Board building on Walnut Street. (WAP.)

The thinkers and planners stand at the foot of Main Street. Near the center of this picture is the highest point in Greenville. Many places a mile or more distant were covered by water as deep as 10 feet or more. (WAP.)

Behind the Levee Board, where Main Street meets the river, are five fire trucks with bells, hoses, and ladders lined up on the levee base. A steamboat's pilothouse and stacks can be seen above the levee. They illustrate the difference in the height of the river on the levee compared with the land side. (WAP.)

In a very short time conditions have changed (same location above). Refugees began arriving on the levee and setting up their makeshift homes for the next month. A raised wooden sidewalk has also been built to accommodate foot traffic. (WAP.)

When the levee broke flood refugees took shelter in the courthouse, gins, and businesses around the county. Most of them were relocated to the levee in Greenville or railroad tracks in Leland. The flood-experienced population knew where to park their cars. (WAP.)

Registered nurse Loree Wall gives a 1927 flood refugee the necessary shots to prevent the spread of diseases, especially typhoid. Everyone was expected to have the inoculations. (WAP.)

Greenville's streets and the country around remained flooded for a month or more after a second rise came. Before the flood the idea of a levees-only policy was in place. After the disaster, flood control engineers began to talk seriously about artificial cutoffs to speed the flood waters past constricted areas such as the Greenville Bends, a series of meandering bends above the town. (WAP.)

There were few amenities on the levee. Refugees lived in either homemade or Red Cross–donated tents and ate at makeshift tables. They were dependent on others for daily necessities. A large floating wooden communal "outhouse" was put in place next to the levee. (WAP.)

In Leland, refugees received food from the kitchen attached to the depot. Many who had experienced floods before brought their own wood-burning stoves to Leland. The stoves were placed in the open and used as private kitchens. (DOB.)

Navy seaplanes checked for weak places in the levee and looked for stranded refugees. This plane has landed near the railroad tracks in Leland. (DOB.)

At Head, north of Leland, a train engine fell into a washout that was 45 feet deep, drowning the engineer. Just two cars behind the engine slept the U.S. Vice President Charles Dawes. Ironically, he never awakened during the incident. Some of the rails were washed three-quarters of a mile away. They were twisted and bent beyond use. (WAP.)

Located 6 miles north of Leland, Head Station, a railroad flag stop in 1927, became the southernmost point of the Yazoo & Mississippi Valley Railroad during the flood. (WAP.)

Helm, 2 miles north of Head Station, became the supply depot for food and feed during the 1927 flood. (WAP.)

Hampton, a stop on the Yazoo & Mississippi Valley Railroad east of Glen Allen, had many buildings including this gin at the time of the 1927 flood. When the railroad ceased to come to Hampton, people moved to Glen Allan.

The Methodist church of Glen Allan is still in use by area members. Mr. P.L. Mann bought the organ, and Mrs. P.L. Mann bought the piano.

Pictured here is the Bank of Glen Allan in 1927 flood.

Repair work to the Mound Crevasse began shortly after the flood. Mules were the main source of power, though a steam dredge works in the right background. (GTC.)

After the flood, both agriculture and business had to rebuild an economic base. The alluvial soil has always been made richer by floodwaters, and the millet crop after the 1927 flood was abundant. (WAP.)

Frank England Sr. established England Motor Company in 1926. It was first located in the Shelton building on Washington and Theobald. After purchasing General Tire, the company was moved to this location at 216 Main Street, currently the Greenville Police Department, but formerly a livery stable. (FE.)

Greenville's tallest building, the Greenville Hotel has had many lives. Built on the bed of old Rattlesnake Bayou, the building's foundation settled and cracked between the old and new addition built in 1938. Tables in the restaurant moved across the floor during the period of the building's settlement. Until the crack's repair, it was Greenville's biggest curiosity. (PA)

The Greenville High School Class of 1927 never graduated. They were "flushed" out of school. The school building on Main Street became part of the E.E. Bass complex when the annex was completed. (WAP.)

The 1930s Winterville school bus to Greenville has pulled to the side of the "concrete sidewalk down the middle of the road," old Highway No. 1. The road was a 9-foot slab of concrete just wide enough for one car. Riding in the bus are, from left to right, Jeff Wilkerson, Caroline Wilkerson, unidentified, and the school bus driver, Mrs. Blanche Keel. At this time, Washington County had more concrete roads than any other county in Mississippi. (WP.)

The Central Junior High ball players, c. 1930, are, from left to right, (seated) H.G. Payne (Tut), P.B. Griffin, Tom Payne, Billy McGhee, Billy Payne, Pete Woods, and Eugene Fisher (Carl); (kneeling) Leverete Stockdale, Henry Posner, Bubba Dugger, S.D. Rowland, and Ira Stull; (standing) Lawrence Hoggett, Charlie Hall, C.P. Gardner, Othello Harper, Jeff Wilkerson, and Coach Clair Coe. (PWN.)

Members of the *Pica* (the Greenville High School newspaper) staff in 1935 are pictured, from left to right, as follows: (front row) Kenneth Haxton, Herman Crowder, Shelby Foote, Jack Trim, and Percy Bell; (second row) Jack Baskin; women (in no particular order) Nancy Trigg, Ethel Wetherbee, Grace Rabinowitz, Frances Kern, and unidentified; and Tom Finlay; (third row) Howard Mitcham, Geneva Morrow, Ione Boudreaux, Sally Kirk, Nell Robertshaw, and Mary Hunt; (back row) Ferd Moyse, Miss Lillian McLaughlin (sponsor), and Cameron Montgomery.

U.S. Highway 82, built in the 1930s, dips under the railroad tracks in Leland, Mississippi. The underpass has long been a landmark of the city. (DBES.)

A three-engine aluminum German Fokker airplane delivered the first airmail to Greenville in 1938. The delivery was a one-time event to shunt the mail pouch. The Greenville's dirt runway was located near Fishlake. From left to right are Ernest Broughton Henderson Jr. (postmaster, 1964–1972), Harold Barclay, Horace Polk (postmaster, 1961–1964), Carl Webber, Marguerite Johnson (postmistress, 1936–1961), Mildred Wing, Hugh "Count" Van Norman, and Robert Dawson. (BH.)

The Greenville front has a more modern look. The old city wharf boat (at right behind the towboat) was used as a port terminal from 1934 to 1959. It had a storage capacity of approximately 8,000 tons, including storage facilities under the deck for 20,000 bushels of grain. The boat was built by Ingalls Iron Works in Chickasaw, Alabama. (PWN.)

Gen. Harley H. Ferguson, appointed president of the River Commission, started the program of cutoffs between the Arkansas and Red Rivers. Three of the five cutoffs were made in the Greenville Bends during the 1930s. Lake Ferguson was named for this river engineer, who removed the river's dangerous current from the town. (WAP.)

The Yacht Club, established in 1937, was a private club on Lake Ferguson that promoted boating, water sports, and fishing. Its founding members were J.S. Kirk, C.P. Williams, Guy Drew, Mat Virden, Pat Barcroft, and William Payne

In 1901 there was one ferry crossing the river between Greenville and Memphis, and it was located at Mound Landing. Greenville began its own ferry service that year to "furnish a way across the river for drovers, settlers and all who desire to cross." (WAP.)

Individual slabs of concrete are loaded on to barges and are tied by hand with cables to make a large mat. The mats are placed on caving banks and areas prone to swift currents to prevent the river from eroding land on the bank that might cause caving or the danger of crevasse.

The first of Mississippi's state parks to be constructed, LeRoy Percy Park was named for Washington County's favorite son—a senator, planter, and civic leader. Located west of Hollandale on Mississippi Highway 12, the park was dedicated on July 26, 1935, having been built by young men who were participating in President Franklin D. Roosevelt's New Deal organization, the Civilian Conservation Corps. (DBES.)

Anglers gathered for the sport of fishing on a part of the old dam at Lake Washington.

Horseracing was a popular sport in the early decades of the 1900s. The Park family transported their racehorses to different tracks in this large van and entered their horses in the sulky races at Greenway Park. A sulky is a light, two-wheeled vehicle accommodating one person and drawn by a single horse. Fire Chief Bill Chipman was a known sulky driver. (MP.)

Miss Leland, also known as "Streak," the jumping horse of Dr. K.L. Witte of Leland, won numerous awards in the 1930s, including a national title in 1938 and a tie for second in the international competition in 1939. Ellis Rivers was the horse's trainer and usual rider. Leland also sponsored horse shows during the era in its so-called "Alfalfa Bowl" stadium. (DBES.)

A gas station in Glen Allan offered good prices, full service, and a smile with every tank full of gas.

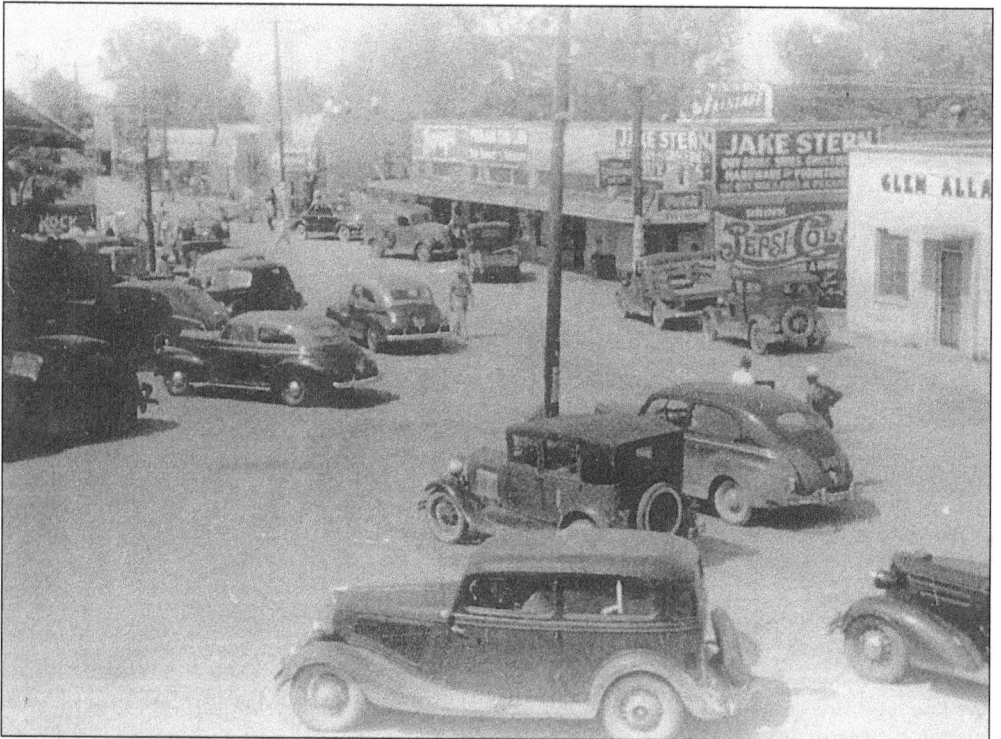

On a Saturday afternoon, Glen Allan offered a chance for the community to get together. The town had a bank, a doctor's clinic, several stores, a cotton gin, and a post office.

Four

WORLD WAR II
AND THE 1940s

When this picture was taken in the 1940s, the building in the center was home to the Greenville *Delta Democrat-Times* newspaper of Hodding Carter. He made the location famous as the title of his book *Where Main Street Meets the River*. The Catholic Church spire is visible on the left, and the opera house is on the right. At the time, parking was at an angle and the old streetlights were still in place. (PWN.)

The Lake (showing *Desire Me* with Greer Garson), the Ritz, and the Paramount were three theaters located in the downtown shopping area in the 1940s. The Lake was near the west end of Washington Avenue. The Ritz and the Paramount were on the southwest corners of Hinds and Broadway, respectively. Drive-in theaters included the Joy, located on the northeast corner of Highway 82 and Beauchamp, and the Anne, located between Leland and Greenville on Highway 82. (WAP.)

Prior to the construction of a bridge over the Mississippi River near Greenville, travelers had to be ferried across the river. Due primarily to the efforts of Greenville Chamber of Commerce secretary John A. Fox in the late 1930s, the two-mile long bridge linking Greenville with Arkansas was officially opened in October 1940. For the first ten years, motorists had to pay a toll to help pay for the structure. Subsequently, the City of Greenville bought the ferry property and discontinued it. (WAP.)

Construction of the airfield at Greenville took place late in 1941. "Greenville Army Air Field," as it was originally called, was created for the training of Army aviators. When completed, there were 144 buildings and 5 runways, including 46 barracks, 11 supply rooms, 12 operations buildings, 5 mess halls, a parachute building, a theater, a chapel, a commissary, a Post Exchange, classrooms, link trainer buildings, and other facilities.

The first training aircraft arrived in Greenville in October 1941, and the first cadre of students arrived on November 16, 1941. The base closed in March 1945 and was used as a standby base. It was reactivated in 1950 as a flying school under civilian contract. The military contingent consisted of about 45 officers and airmen. In March 1953 the base's mission changed and it operated as a jet training facility until 1960. From 1960 to 1964, it was a non-flying technical training base, and in 1966, the site finally closed.

During the early years of the 1930s, a group of Baptist ladies visited with Chinese families in their homes and invited them to come to services at the First Baptist Church. The first Chinese Mission began in 1934. Chinese immigrants came to the Delta after the War between the States as replacements for the African-American laborers who were leaving at that time. (SN.)

Before 1945, Chinese children attended a separate school that had one room and just one teacher working with all the grade levels. First admitted to junior and senior high schools, Chinese residents in the area would be admitted into the lower grades over the course of the next few years. Mrs. E.B. Reynolds is pictured here with the young students in her class of 1946–1947. (WAP.)

During World War II, 20,000 captured German troops were shipped to Mississippi. In 1944, branch camps were set up at Greenville, Leland, and Camp Elkas on Lake Washington. A few prisoners elected to remain in the community after the war.

At Camp Elkas a prisoner's day began at 5:30 a.m. They were allowed 30 minutes to shave, which was followed by breakfast. Their workday lasted from 8 a.m. until 4 p.m., and "lights out" was at 9 p.m. Prisoners received 80¢ a day that was paid in canteen scrip and deposit slips.

In April 1945 Brown's Pastry Shop made pies, cakes, and cookies by hand. The pie crusts were rolled thin by a machine, and the cookies were rolled with a large pin. Owned by African Americans, the business was considered the best place in Greenville to buy pastries. (WAP.)

Coleman High School's homecoming queen, Polly Ann Terry, poses with her court in 1949, while a small marching band waits behind them. The event took place at Sportsman Field at the corner of Wilson and Union. This field was the home of the Greenville Bucks (Buckshot) baseball team. Other teams in the Negro League were the Memphis Red Socks, the Indianola Clowns, and the Black Barons. Famous visitors to the field included Jackie Robinson, Willie Mays, and Satchel Page. (WAP.)

Candidates for baptism sit on the front row at St. John's Church. Members of the Mother Board, a position of honor given to older women in the congregation, sit on the right side behind the children.

The congregation of the new Mount Zion Church represents the many small churches that have disappeared across the Delta. Standing on its roof with a hammer and yardstick is Rev. W.C. Chester, who was also the builder of the church.

Originally, Do's Restaurant, or Doe's, was a grocery store in an African-American neighborhood. In the early 1940s, it changed from being strictly a black "honky tonk" in the front of the store, serving buffalofish and chili, to a restaurant, to later serving tamales to the "carriage trade" (white, upper-class customers) at the back door because of segregation. Politicians, actors, and everyday people have driven many miles to have dinner at Doe's. (PWN.)

"Big Doe Signa" began Doe's Restaurant, which has a tradition of serving 3-pound T-bone steaks and 4- to-5-pound sirloins. The restaurant remains virtually unchanged since the 1940s. (PWN.)

George Hampton Uzzelle, the owner of Peru Plantation, is seen here in 1952. He had about 1,500 head of Black Angus cattle.

Clifford (Cliff) Kelly Brown was a true cowboy. He could rope any cow by either foot and tell you beforehand which foot he was going to rope. He managed cattle for George Hampton Uzzelle on Peru Plantation.

Five

DELTA FOLKS

A future successful businessman and planter (LeRoy Percy), a Civil War historian (Shelby Foote), and a philosopher (Walker Percy) enjoy some leisure time in the garden of their uncle and friend (William A. Percy). (WAP.)

William Alexander Percy is an enigma to many. He was simply a gifted writer, a caring citizen, and a leader of the Washington County community. He had a strong sense of family, which he demonstrated by adopting his nephews, Walker, LeRoy, and Phinizy. *Lanterns on the Levee*, his biography, tells the story of his growing up in Washington County. (WAP.)

Known by the pen name Ellen Douglas, Josephine Haxton has lived in many Southern states. Her writings include short stories, poems, essays, and magazine articles. Her latest book, *Truth: Four Stories I Am Finally Old Enough to Tell*, has many recognizable Southern characters. (WAP.)

Bern Keating has lived in Greenville since 1946 but, because of his interest in writing about travel and history, could easily find his way around Paris. His works include over 30 books and articles that have appeared in *National Geographic*, *Smithsonian*, and other travel magazines. He and his wife, Frankie, are also noted photographers. (BK.)

Ellis Brooks Haxton, the youngest son of Josephine and Kenneth, has published eight books of poetry. Many of his poems reflect his youth in Greenville. (WAP.)

Kenneth Haxton, a native of Greenville, has many talents. He has constructed and sold over 300 crossword puzzles to the *New York Times*, the publisher Simon and Schuster, and other publications and has composed over 150 musical works, including two piano concerti and two symphonies. His most recently published novel, *The Undiscovered Territory*, is set in his hometown. (KH.)

Willie Foster grew up singing the blues on Dunleith Plantation near Stoneville. His instrument is the "harp" (harmonica), and he played for many years in juke joints around Greenville and Indianola. His band is called the Rhythm and Blues Upsetters. (BR.)

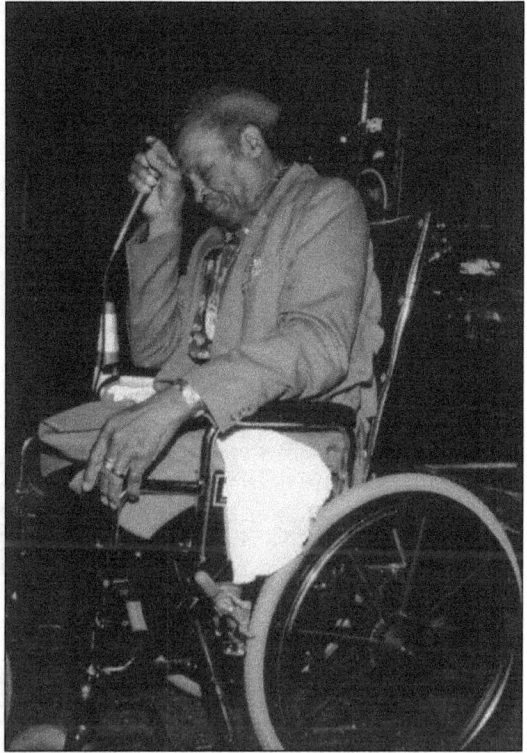

James "Son" Thomas worked as a gravedigger before becoming a blues singer. He toured and recorded his music in Germany. The film *Gateway to the Delta: Delta Blues Singer James (Sonny Ford) Thomas* won the Mississippi Arts film festival award in 1972. He is buried in Bogue Cemetery. (JK.)

Boogaloo Ames was celebrated as a pianist and band leader in the 1940s Detroit jazz scene. Eden Brent has worked with Boogaloo for 15 years, and they recently performed at the Kennedy Center and the 2000 Republican National Convention in Philadelphia, Pennsylvania. (AR.)

Pictured on the left, Eugene Powell, or "Sonny Boy Nelson," a self-taught guitarist, could play rhythm, lead, and bass at the same time. Sam Chatmon, at right, of Hollandale is considered to be among the most important figures in American music. His contributions helped create the lyrical art form of the blues. Here the pair perform at the Delta Blues Festival held near Greenville in the early 1980s. Chatmon is buried in Hollandale, and Powell in Metcalfe. (BR.)

Jim Henson was born in Greenville and grew up in Leland. His father worked as research scientist at Stoneville. While playing on the banks of Deer Creek, Jim conceived the idea of "Kermit the Frog," the first of his Muppet creations.

Washington County—"The most Southern place on earth." (Henson.)

Because both Old (1847) and New Greenville (1865) were established on the Mississippi River, the town has suffered constantly from the threat of caving into the river. Controlling the devastating effects of the river became the first priority of settlers. In 1898, when the Corps of Engineers completed the present levee at Greenville, Walnut Street became the first city street to parallel the river. Front, First, Mulberry, and Locust Streets were buried beneath the levee and are now in Lake Ferguson. (WAP.)